PILGRIM

VOLUME 1

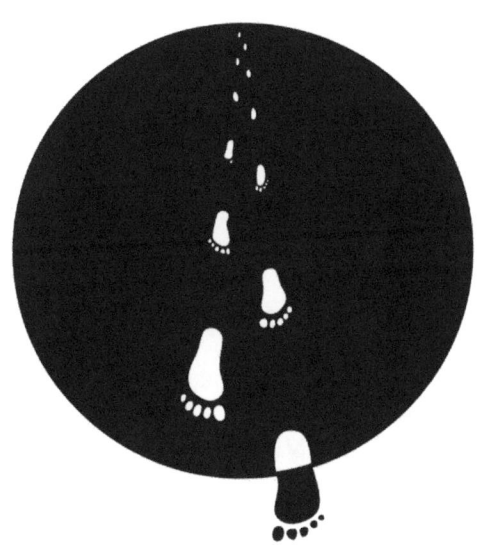

FRANK PREM & LEANNE MURPHY

Publication Details

Published by Wild Arancini Press
Copyright © 2024 Frank Prem & Leanne Murphy

All rights reserved:
No part of this publication may be reproduced, stored in a retrieval system, or transmitted in any form or by any means, electronic, mechanical, photocopying, recording or otherwise, without prior written permission from the publisher and author.

Title: Pilgrim: Volume 1
ISBN: 978-1-923166-10-3 (pbk)
ISBN: 978-1-923166-15-8 (e-bk)

Contents

sleep on	5
journey in a new day	7
what it takes	9
natural waiting	11
the dancers	13
the choice of love	15
reaching stars	17
by chance the sea and sky	19
grasp of a paradigm	21
use of vacuum	23
light from other worlds	25
individual difference	27
singular majesty	29
a simple wish	31
unity	33
coo into the wind	35
identification	37
conundrum	39
a doubt of happiness	41

fulfilment	43
elemental alchemy	45
by blood belonging	47
principled lines	49
choosing	51
escape power	53
when it is sufficient	55
time	57
simple revelation	59
the teacher	61
lone states	63
the power of air	65
progress	67
time and barricades	69
freely given	71
awareness in the air	73
return to heal	75
enough is enough	77
un-sound universe	79
walk through heaven	81
dark concept	83
unwrapping	85

the future now	87
thought shapes	89
thought sound	91
a peak above forgiveness	93
the right task	95
homecoming	97
vision	99
who changes	101

to you
fellow pilgrim

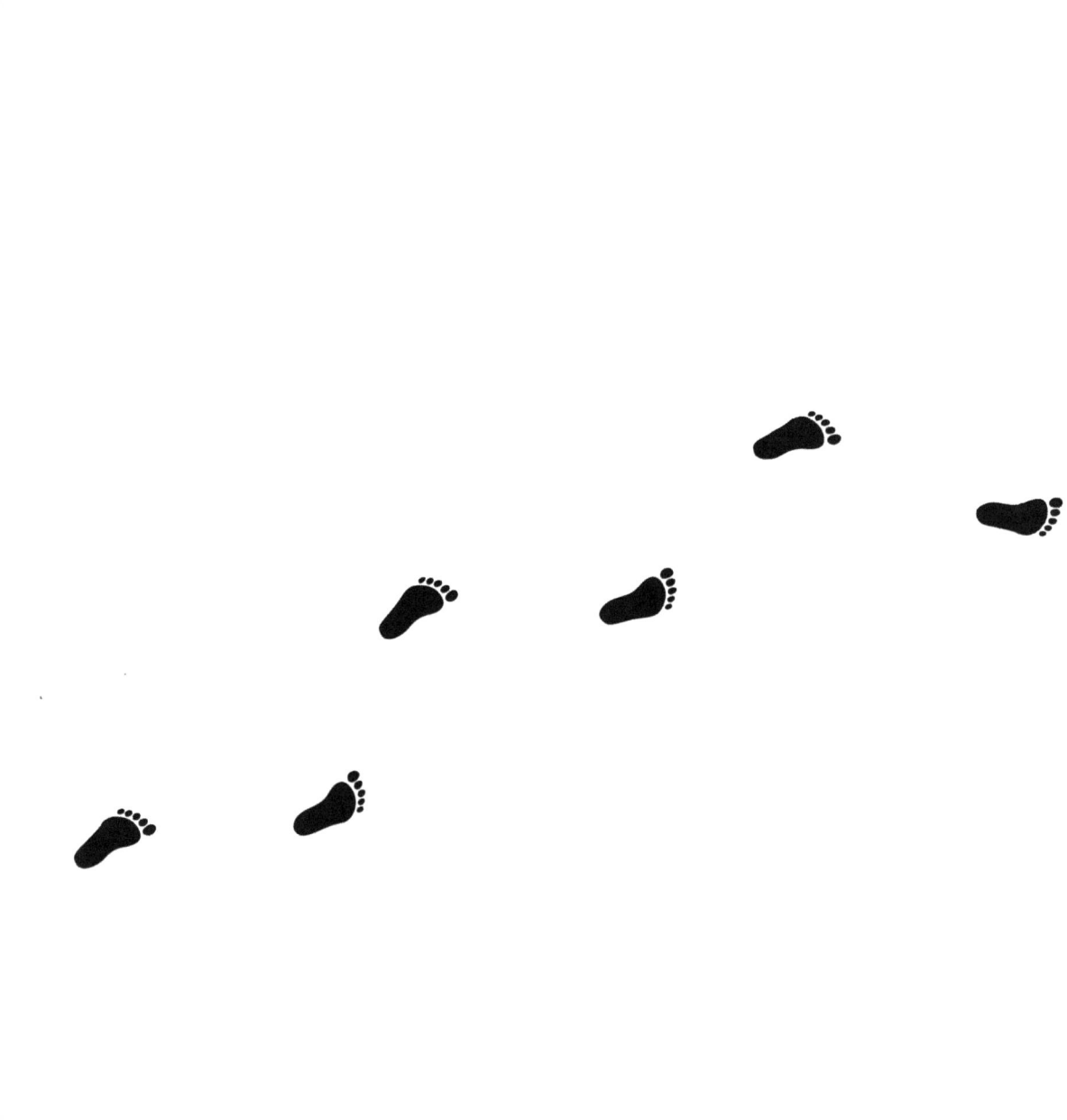

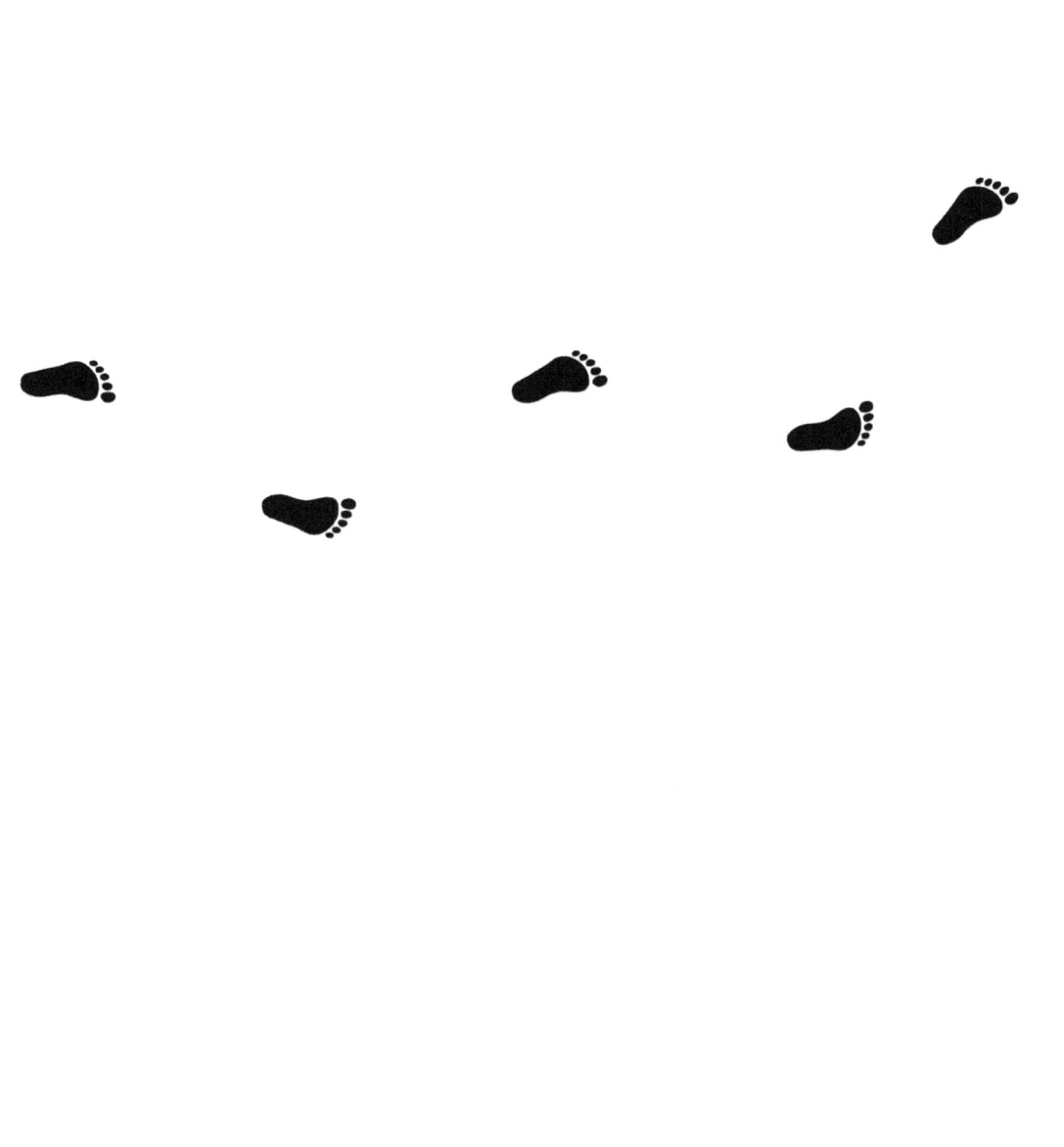

scant sighting

pilgrim
do not weep

this is a journey
that passes
almost within sight
and truly
you may catch
a fleeting glimpse

yes
even you might catch
a glimpse
before the shadows
draw a veil

did you think
there would be
more

sometimes it seems
overrated
other times as though
hardly there

better
if you keep your eyes down
your mind focused
on the road
for your footsteps
will leave their own mark
in the dust behind you

consider
might not that
be enough

do not weep
pilgrim
this journey
is just a glimpse

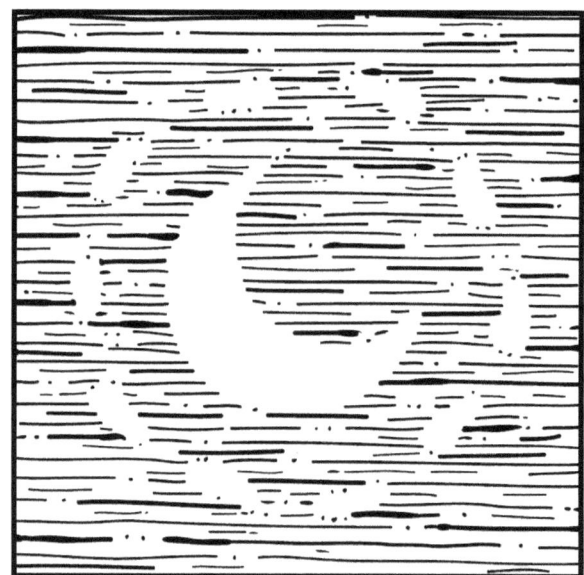

sleep on

do not listen too hard
to your dreams
pilgrim
you should know
you will not stop travelling
simply because of slumber

dreams
are a chance perceived

every night
a new gamble

you will not always know
if you've won or lost
or what they mean
but

dreams will lay the way
in mist and smoke
before you

stay true
to your heart
do not surrender
your good reasons
or shy
from a troubled moment

for in these restless visions
meaning
may be obscured

pilgrim
sleep on
dream your chances

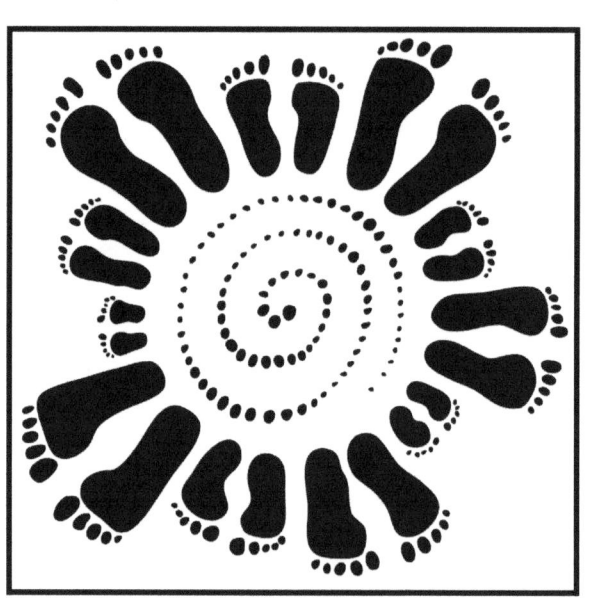

journey in a new day

pilgrim
hold your head up
it is not permitted to sink low
beyond redeeming
don't cast your gaze upon the ground

the journey is fresh-begun
each day
tomorrow is for new steps
another road

pilgrim
lift your gaze

the sun is rising

what it takes

it only costs a little pity
to cry
pilgrim

all it takes
is a small space
inside
your heart

let it beat loudly

for all it takes
is a pity

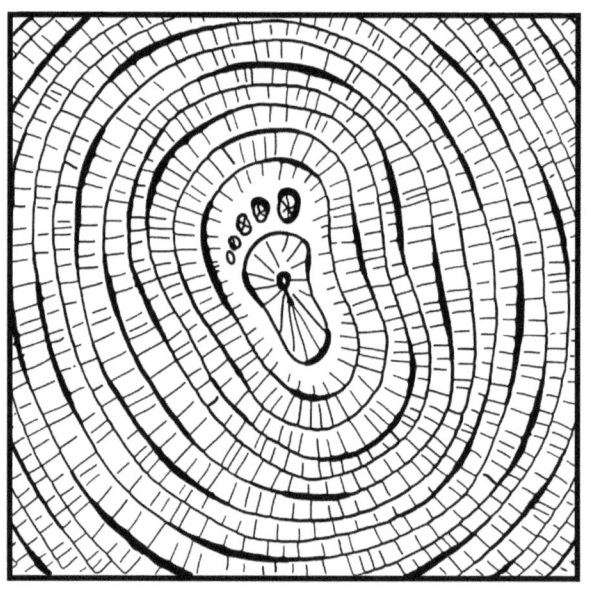

natural waiting

everyone must wait
pilgrim

was that not made clear
before now

this is the nature of time
and what is a life
but time
spent

waiting

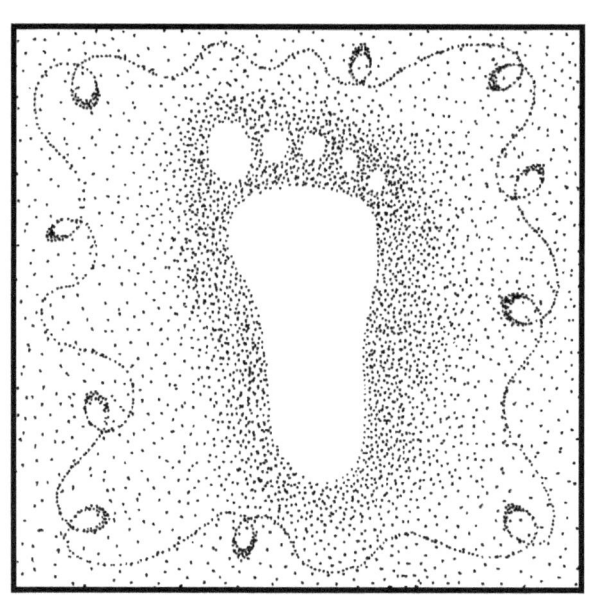

the dancers

there are some
pilgrim
who glide and dance
their elegance
unsurpassed

they hold gifts of grace
in the way that they move

to watch them
is to mingle with certainty

but you
my traveller
can place your footsteps
in dirt
to raise a cloud of dust
and move without fetter

this too may count
as a salvation

the choice of love

yes
of course you will encounter love
pilgrim

it is needed
to shape your heart

you may break
from what you learn
and yet grow
while the innocence
of a child
remains within

the guidance is fate
but the learning is yours
to embrace

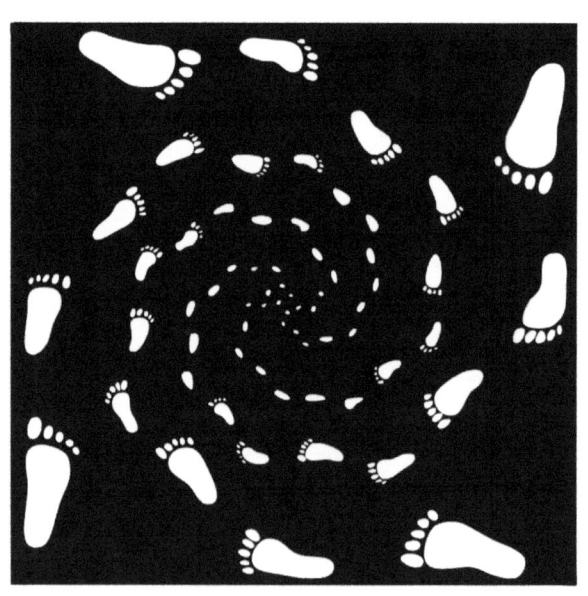

reaching stars

yes pilgrim
there is a way to the stars

it is right that you should wonder

their placement beyond immediate grasp
is a function of awe
the creation of a light
for aspiration

when you *know*
you may wish to reach and touch
hold them in the soft palm
of your hand

but ask yourself
if you knew
would that still be your need

or should they stay
an inspiration in your mind
where they began

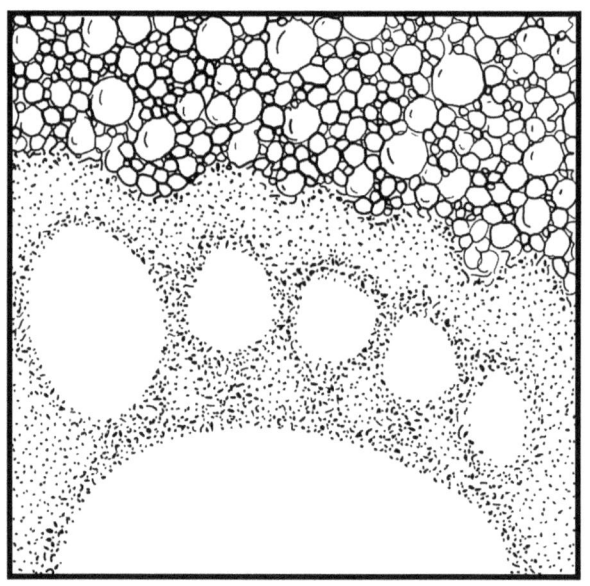

by chance the sea and sky

   o sea

I call

   o sky

  with grains of sand
  make me clean

  scour me
  I would be pure
  before the night falls

pilgrim
do not forget
that each grain
has a purpose

there is no
greater reason

no larger task
than to be cleansed
by passing
through the elements

none
will be met
by chance

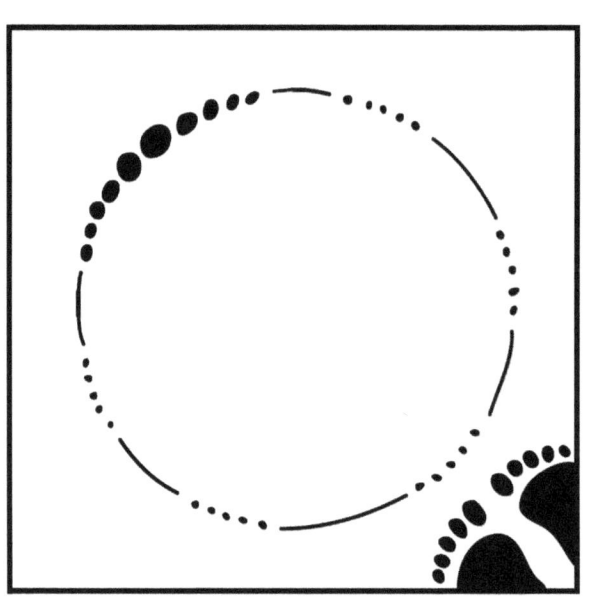

grasp of a paradigm

do you long
pilgrim
for fresh comprehension

a new paradigm
that might hold *all*
the entire cosmos as you know it

a place where
your existence
could be understood

do not distress yourself
over perspective

it is fundamental
to the nature of possibility
that answers will shimmer
at the periphery
of vision

use of vacuum

pilgrim
each departure
offers an opportunity

consider

in the immediate vacuum
are the sparkling lights
of reflection
and understanding

take these moments
immerse yourself
in the process of review

then move forward

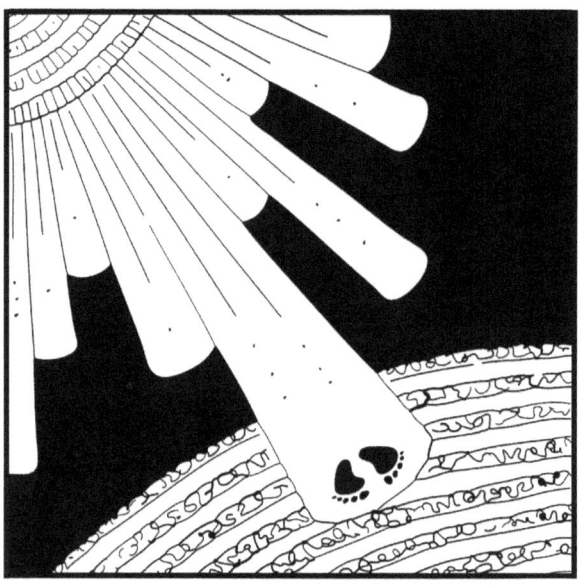

light from other worlds

there are other worlds
pilgrim
beyond the space you inhabit

when you see the rim of the sun
rise
shimmering
above the horizon

when you see a single fall of light
radiant
reach from the sky to the earth

are you not compelled
to believe

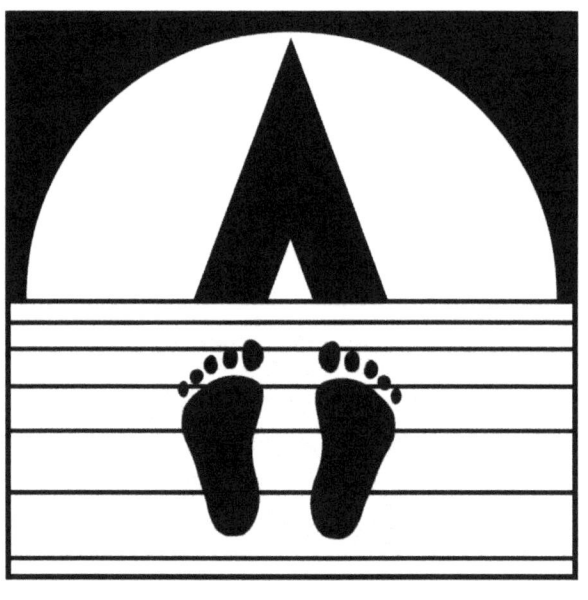

individual difference

each encounter
is an entry into a new world
pilgrim

these worlds are as many
and as different
as your mind can conceive

and truly *your* world
is unlike any other you will meet

does this not make you
unique

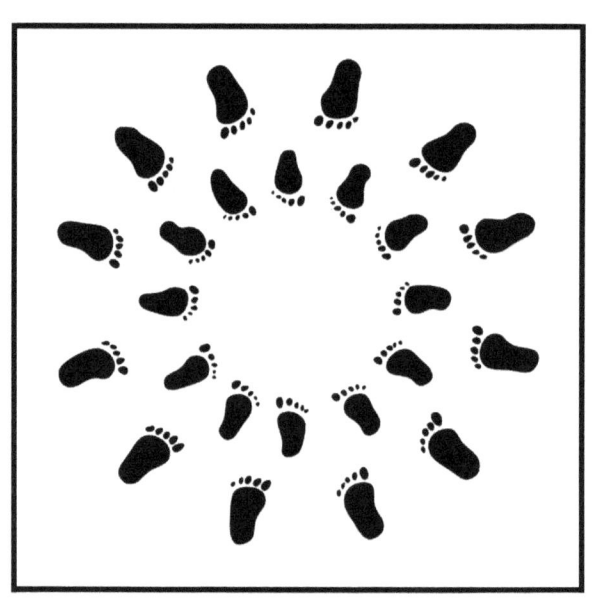

singular majesty

ah pilgrim
of course it is right
to talk of the existence of god

look around you
there is a reason
for beauty

to speak of *a* god
however
seems less than just
to the majesty
of creation

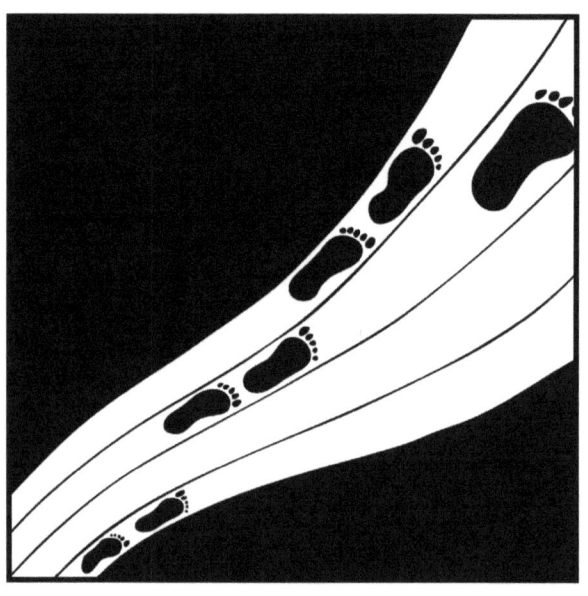

a simple wish

consider
pilgrim
when you make a wish
what is it you are seeking

is it the fulfilment
of desire

perhaps
a prayer for guidance

correction of error

strength
to achieve expectations

was there ever something
so simple
as the making of a wish

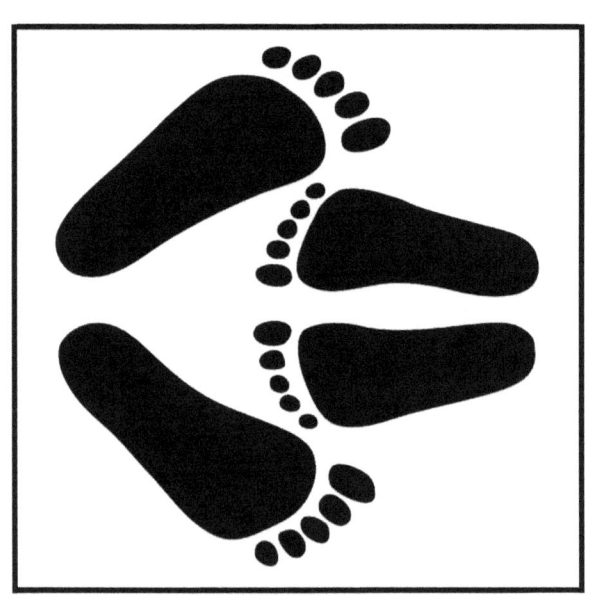

unity

in your lovers arms
pilgrim
do you find joy

know peace

is your lover an extension
of yourself

should you find the place
of release
you will be as one

grow together
pilgrim

share this joy

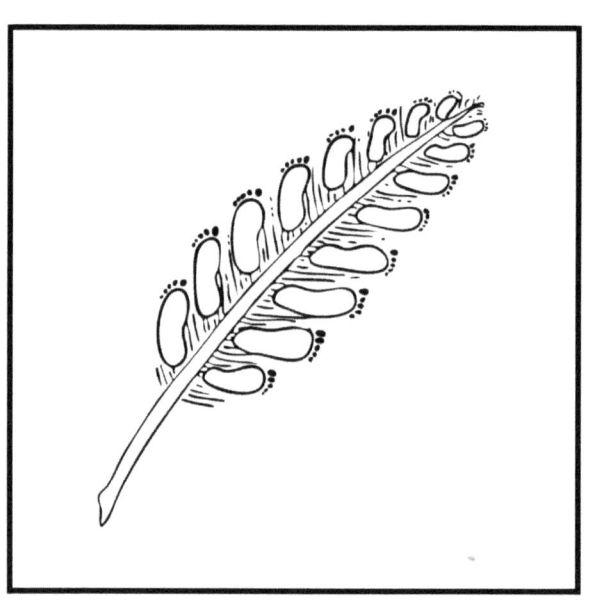

coo into the wind

the pigeon sings
a constant *cooing* song
while it raises nestlings

the two birds
share their duties
devoted to the task

but there comes a time
when their attention
turns
and they feel the urge
to begin again

what then
for the nestlings
pilgrim

it is not always
an easy thing
to search
for your own path

yet
neither will it be found
beneath the feathers
and wings
of your birthplace

turn your face
to the wind
pilgrim

then fly

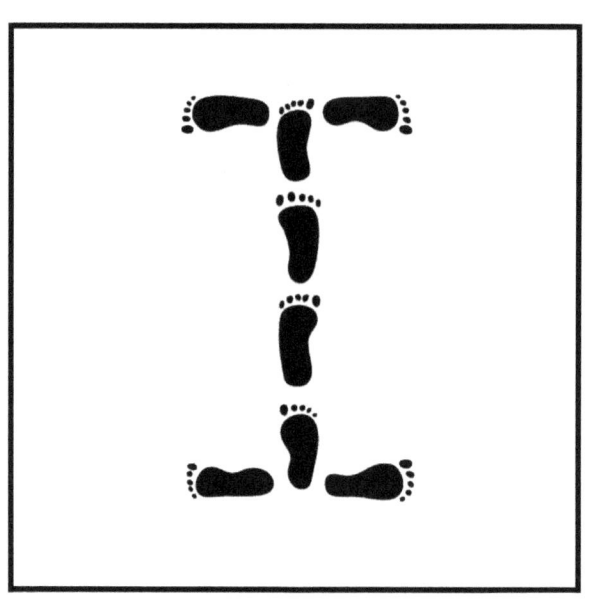

identification

what is it about names
pilgrim

have you wondered

we come into this world
and are spoken aloud

from this

identity

when you come to choose
for yourself

who then
will you be

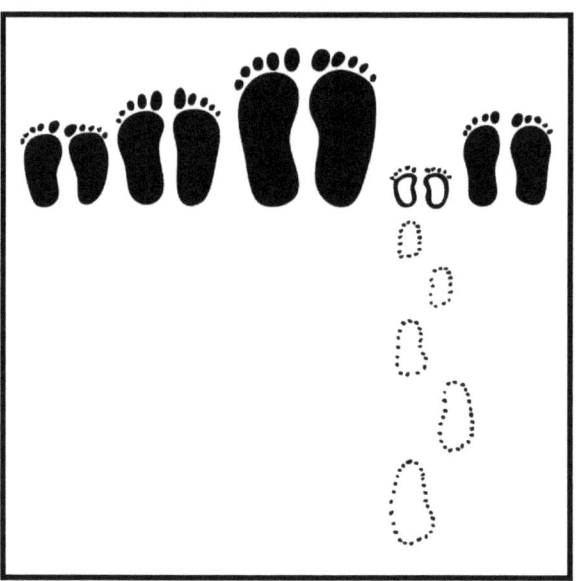

conundrum

honesty is a currency
pilgrim

it will buy you entry
to places otherwise barred
no matter
the coinage offered

the pain that comes
when you are rebuffed
is the shock
of the unexpected
for
what honest person
would anticipate
mistrust

and therein
lies the conundrum
pilgrim
for the only response
is honesty
yet again

do not despair at this
but know
trust can only be purchased
a single truth
at a time

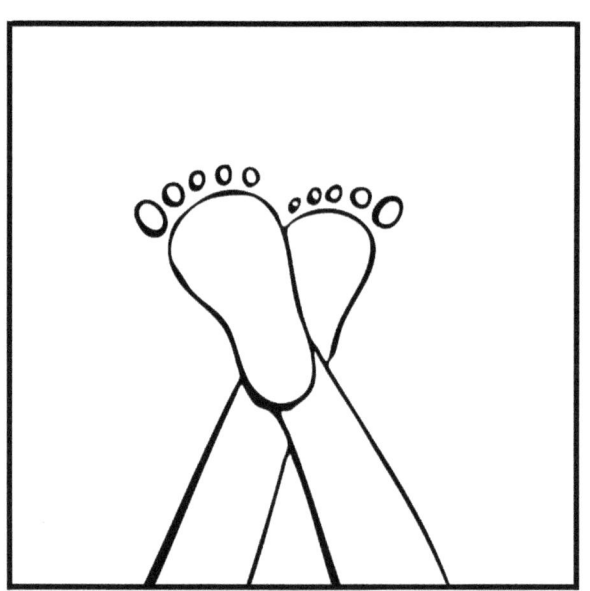

a doubt of happiness

when you see a person
who is happy
pilgrim
are you not led to think
in terms of the positive
as though happiness
is itself a presence

consider
happiness may actually be a negative
marked by an absence
of questions

isn't it possible
that the positive side of happiness
is overrated
while the joyous wonder
of freedom from doubt
lacks the recognition
deserved

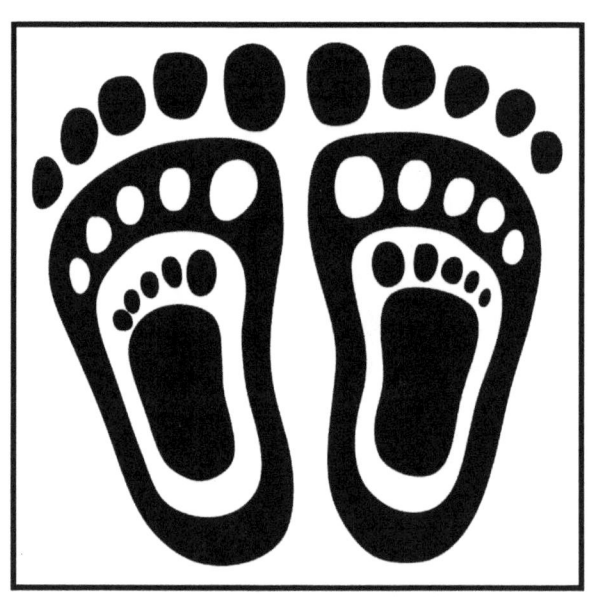

fulfilment

oh pilgrim
there is so much splendour
here

you and I
are mere wayfarers
through this mystery

we walk
with awe and wonder

and if . . .

if there is a purpose
beyond simply passing
this way
then that will evolve

solving such mysteries
is not our task

it is not a factor
in the fulfilment
of destiny

elemental alchemy

there is more
beneath the sky
pilgrim
than air and water
fire and earth

alchemy is inspired
beyond the limitations
of coarse elements

listen to the sound
of your inner self
when you contemplate
your transformation

and know
this too
is an elemental magic

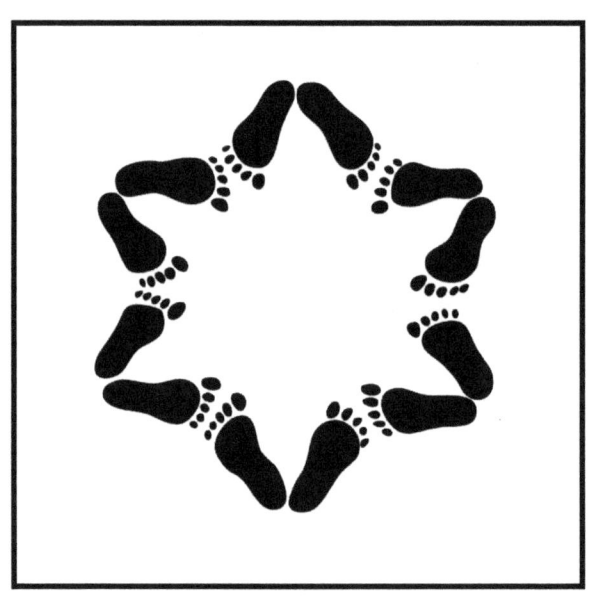

by blood belonging

there are understandings
pilgrim
that evolve
in communion with those
who reared you

with whom you have learned
your way of breaking bread

these are the ones
whose hearts beat
with familiar blood

and so

and so

wherever such a table
is set
your belonging is assured

principled lines

there is a time
pilgrim
to draw your line
in the sand

without knowledge
of the question
an answer will arise
from within you to say

> *here*

> *it is enough*

> *this is where I stand*

how strange
how strong
that compulsion to force
response
before awareness

this line comes
from your principles
from the place
where resides the good
in your moral heart

make your stand
and draw your line
deep and clear

comprehend who you are
pilgrim
know the ground
that you must hold

choosing

have you noticed
pilgrim
each question that confronts you
seems to have
more than one answer

by your choices
you will be made

by your choices
measured

escape power

around us
is what seems to be
noise and movement

the busy-ness of urgent action
shouted loud
until it is inescapable

and yet

when thought is turned
inward
it is possible to find solitude
and tranquility

to perform this inversion
pilgrim
is to exercise power

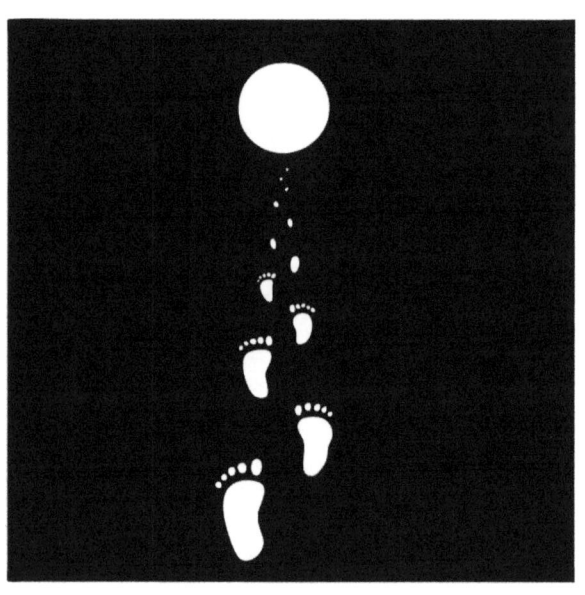

when it is sufficient

it is acknowledged as fact
pilgrim
that at all times
somewhere in this worldly illusion
the sun is shining

there are days
when it is enough
to be pointed towards the light

and to move
with a forward motion

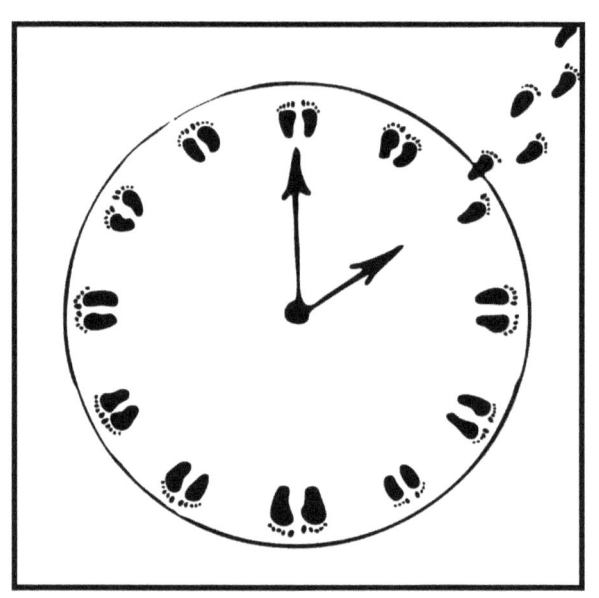

time

oh pilgrim
the days seem long to you
I know

weeks and months pass
with the only sign
of change
a progression in the season

do not despair

the universe is not a party
to haste
and all that must be
will come to be

in time

simple revelation

there is such a thing
as faith
pilgrim

unadorned
and without demonstration
it is a by-word
for acceptance

a man can believe
through all of his life
without
a single proof

how is that so

who can tell

but when you are ready
you will know

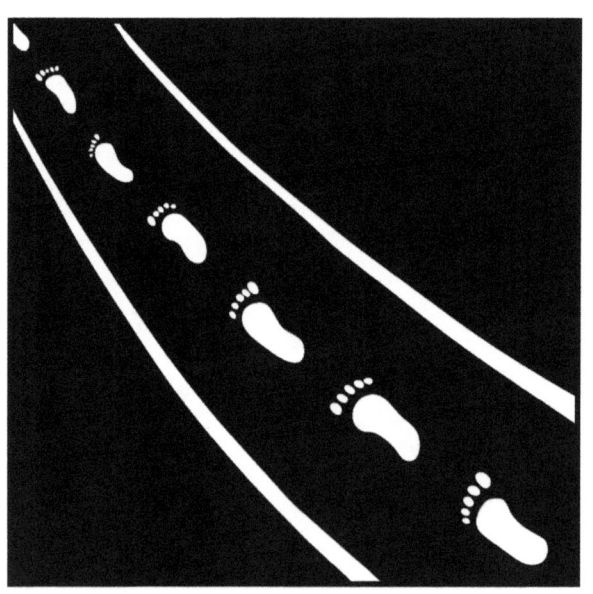

the teacher

the road is a perfect teacher
for you
pilgrim

every day
it carries you to new experiences

until you recognise
that every new thing
is the same

walk the road
and learn

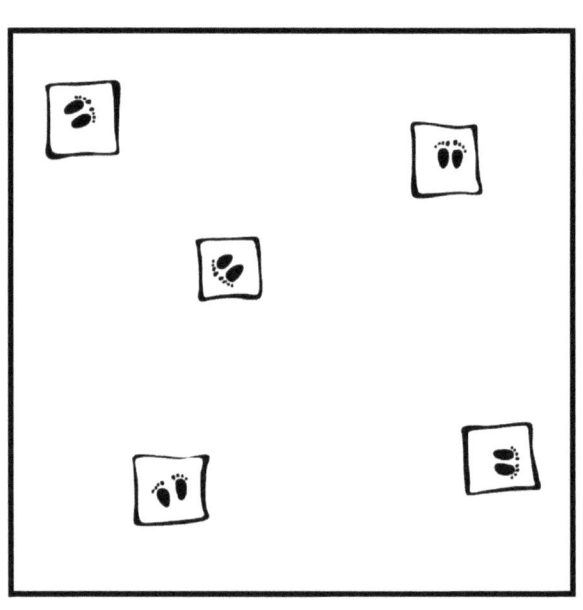

lone states

pilgrim
to be lonely
is an exercise
of endurance

to be alone
is to exercise
choice

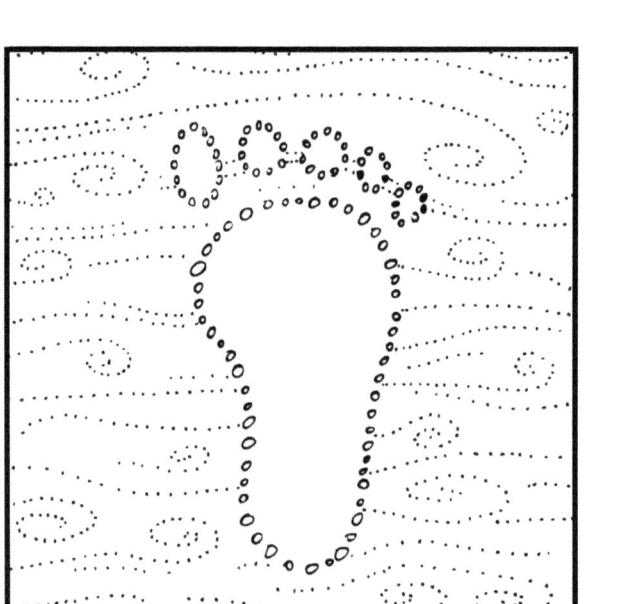

the power of air

raise your hand above your head
pilgrim
close it to make a fist

what have you caught

is it nothing

is it the wind

there is no substance to see
or touch and yet
it felt substantial

this is the way of air
this is the elusive nature
of power

nothing
is something
pilgrim

it was ever so

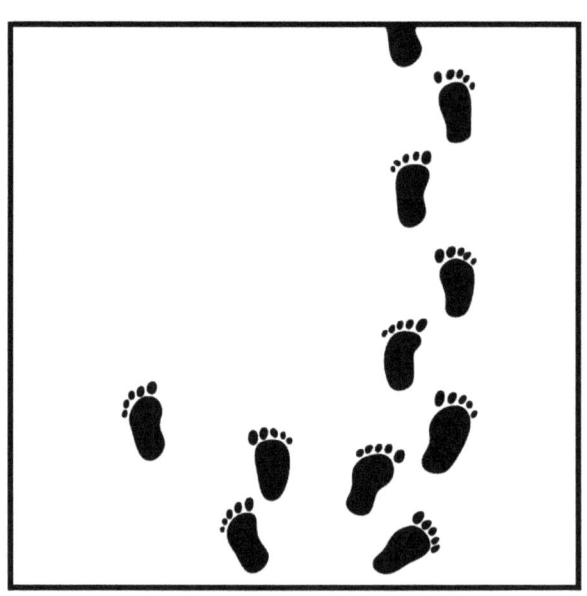

progress

it is not always prudent
to go forward
pilgrim

sometimes it is necessary
to step to the side
or go back
in order to proceed

when you find it timely
to retreat
draw from the familiarity
of known ground

then look forward
again
with refreshed clarity
about yourself
and your purposes

time and barricades

well
pilgrim
it is possible
to erect barricades
that stand tall
and span wide

these may seem successful
for long periods

the passage of time
and illumination by hindsight
however
allow such barriers to be seen
in truer perspective

only then
will the opportunity
to grow beyond
be yours to embrace

freely given

pilgrim
before you question
the apparent absence of gratitude
is there not also an unknown
concerning yourself

if your own gift
is so worthy
as to demand an offering in return
perhaps
just perhaps
it should never
have been given
in the first place

awareness in the air

when the time comes
pilgrim
you will feel it

change is marked
in many ways
sometimes
in the air you breathe
sometimes
the trembling
in your gut
that seems to have
no cause

only rarely
by a clarity of thought
and awareness
of greater purpose
or meaning

when change beckons
you will know

it is then
that your challenge
will begin

return to heal

centre with periphery

hearth with home

reunion is an opportunity
pilgrim

beneath the simplicity
of welcome return
each departure
at its closure
is a chance to make whole
again
that which has been fractured

look into the heart
of your next returning
pilgrim
embrace the occasion
to heal

enough is enough

pilgrim
to the question
when does the journey end

there is no answer

the way is eternal
and the directions
infinite
for those
who wish to travel

and yet
the question demands
determination

it may well be now
pilgrim

the moment to declare
enough

as the shadowed
questions
are replaced
by a quiet illumination
of contentment

perhaps
that moment
is *now*

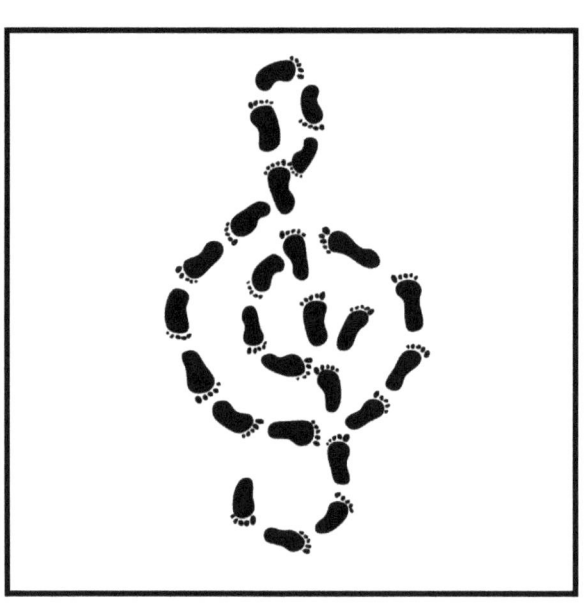

un-sound universe

what is the sound of the universe
pilgrim
have you heard it

how do you know
when
you have heard it

does the sound come
from outside
or within

do not mistake the clacking
of your thoughts
for the song of the cosmos
pilgrim
the universe does not think

it *sings*

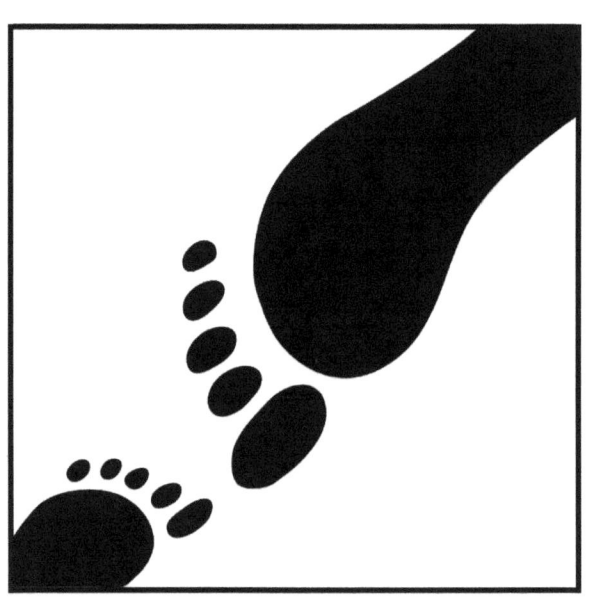

walk through heaven

it is not necessary
to believe in anything
more
than the blue sky
pilgrim

the light extends itself
regardless
to the earth
on which you stand

walk through heaven
and rejoice

dark concept

call the light up
pilgrim
to fathom the darkness

it is an unending well
whose depths begin
at the periphery of sight

always
at the edges
dark aura begins
and a passage between realms
might be something more
than concept

unwrapping

it is sometimes said
pilgrim
that the *self*
has the greatest need
to be unwrapped

over time confusion has emerged
regarding that which is presented
that which is gift
that which is . . .
all

when I present you
with my gift
know as you remove the layers
of pretty crinkled paper
that what I have offered
is an aspect

the future now

the future runs ahead
pilgrim

it expands
like the universe
to every possible point
of each possible compass

now
is a temporary label
that fills each moment
for all of every day

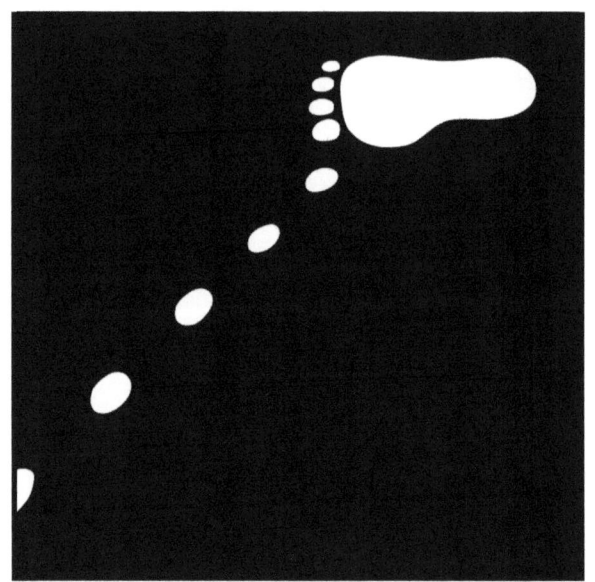

idea shapes

they are shaped with ideas
pilgrim

pondered into condensations
of white matter

of grey portent
stretched into tresses
they are impressions
of a concept of precipitation

clouds of the mind
are harbingers
of a storm of ideas

embrace your weather

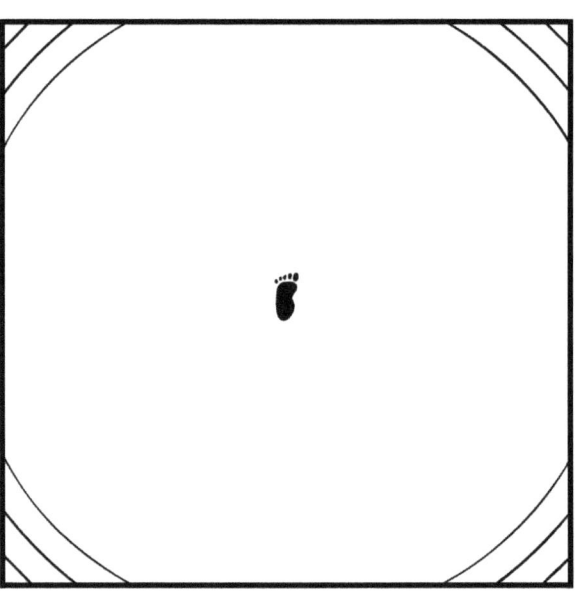

thought sound

listen pilgrim
do you hear
the stillness

even the sound
of a cicada
is embraced
in the silence

becomes the sound
of your thoughts

be still

be still

still

be

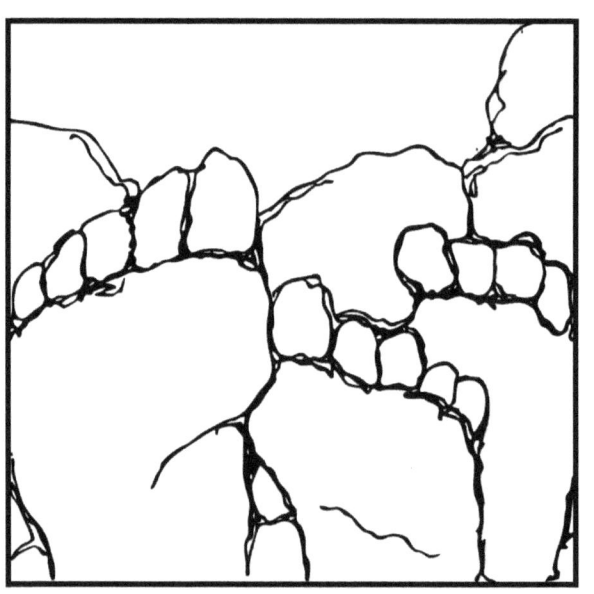

a peak above forgiveness

forgiveness

it has become
fashionable
correct

virtuous

but consider
pilgrim
is forgiveness not
passivity

there are fine points
of distinction
in the mountains
that range between
forgiveness
and restoration

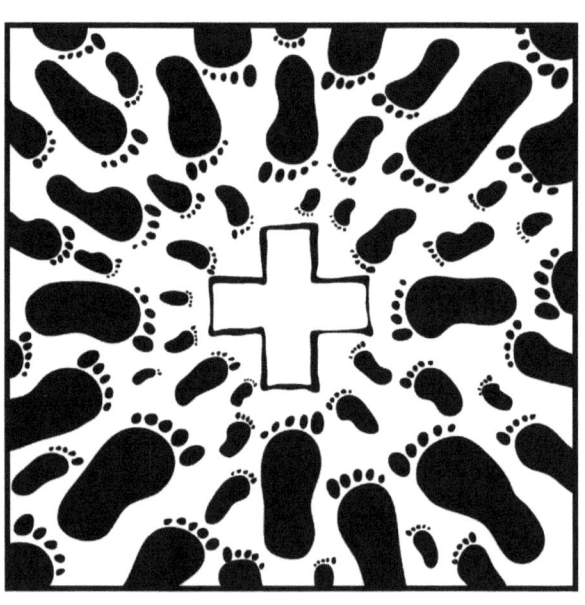

the right task

this world
is the swirling multitude
pilgrim

how many
can you help
towards happiness

how many
before you have performed
sufficient duty

perhaps it is not your task
to help

perhaps
it falls to you
only to leave none
lessened
by your passing

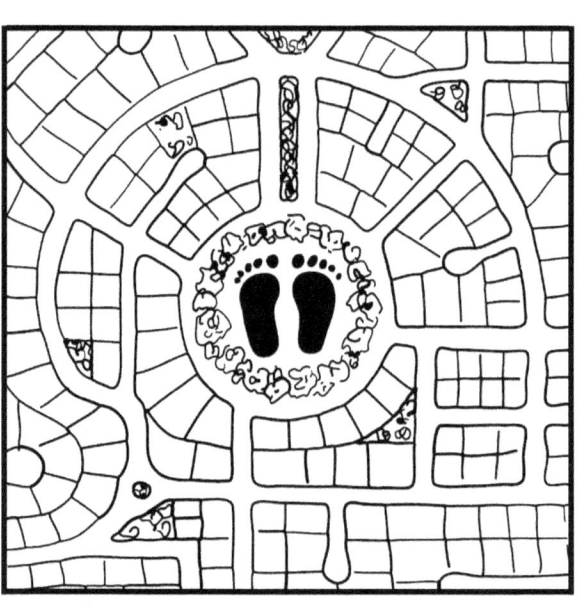

homecoming

home is a place
within you
pilgrim

you might spend your lifetime
searching wide and far
but in truth
it is right where you stand

when your weariness compels you
at last
to end your searching
look within

I will rejoice for you

vision

look around you
pilgrim
is every colour
not the same

broken up
split apart
then reassembled
for you to see
in your own way

the vision is yours

your task
is to see

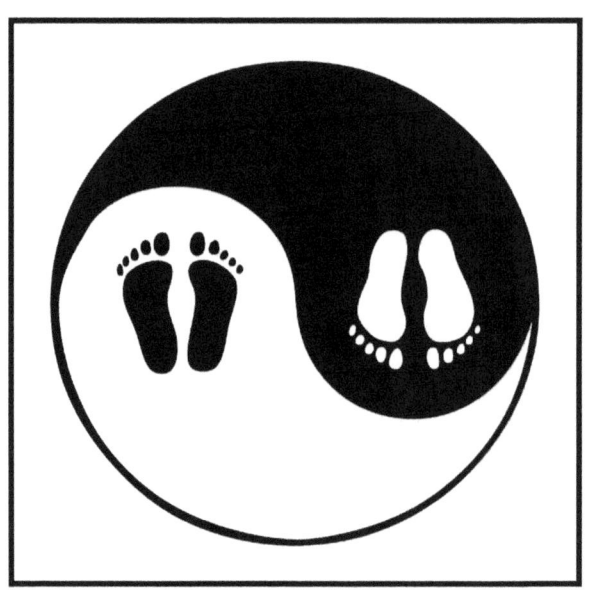

who changes

every *thing* changes
pilgrim
every *one*

even you have changed
within the course
of this journey

we are what we were
and yet
are different from that now
with further alteration to come

are you the one you saw
in the mirror yesterday

who will you be
tomorrow

Frank Prem has been a storytelling poet since his teenage years and a psychiatric nurse through all of his professional career, which now exceeds forty years.

He has been published in magazines, online zines and anthologies in Australia and overseas, and has both performed and recorded his work as spoken word at festivals, community events and workshops.

His other published works include *Small Town Kid, Devil In The Wind* and *The New Asylum* among others.

He lives with Leanne in the beautiful township of Beechworth in north-east Victoria, Australia.

www.FrankPrem.com

Leanne Murphy is a musician, educator, myotherapist, outdoor enthusiast and award-winning artist.

She has been teaching music in many different settings for over three decades and published her first book of original songs in 2023, *Singing The Gold: Songs For Community Volume 1*.

Leanne also spent a number of years touring as a children's puppeteer and developing the craft of captivating young hearts and minds. This earlier training now informs much of her performing and visual art practice.

She lives with Frank and happily wanders the many tracks within the Shire of Indigo and beyond.

www.LeanneMurphy.com.au

www.ingramcontent.com/pod-product-compliance
Lightning Source LLC
Chambersburg PA
CBHW051352110526
44591CB00025B/2982